HAUNTS AND HORRORS

Meghan Gottschall

Haunts and Horrors
Death Uncovered

Full Tilt Press
42964 Osgood Road
Fremont, CA 94539
readfulltilt.com

Full Tilt Press publications may be purchased for educational, business, or sales promotional use.

Editorial Credits
Design and layout by Sara Radka
Edited by Nikki Ramsay
Copyedited by Renae Gilles and Kristin Russo

Image Credits
Getty Images: 500px Plus, 21, 500px Prime, 29, arsenik, 43 (top), D-Keine, 22, David Clapp, 26, EyeEm, 9, 42, iStockphoto, 8 (bottom), iStockphoto, cover, 10, 12, 16, 24, 28, 30, 43 (bottom), kool99, 20, Vulture Labs, 40; Newscom: Christian Kober/robertharding, 36, Ken Welsh, 38, Liszt Collection, 41, MCT/Sacramento Bee/ Manny Crisostomo, 32 (top), 34, 35; Pixabay: Free-Photos, 5, LeoderLiebe, 1, Niedec, background (parchment), Parker_West, 45 (ghost), rawpixel, 45 (book), background (concrete), shrikeshmaster, 3; Wikimedia: Alexander Gardner, 15, Doug Kerr, 18, Infrogmation of New Orleans, 6, National Portrait Gallery London, 39, Smerdis of Tlön 8 (top), Taber Photographic Co., 32 (bottom), United Nations Information Office, New York, 14, Unknown, 27

ISBN: 978-1-62920-808-4 (library binding)
ISBN: 978-1-62920-816-9 (ePUB eBook)

CONTENTS

Haunts and Horrors 4

Voodoo Priestess Marie Laveau 6

White House Ghosts 12

The Amityville Haunting 18

The Bell Witch 24

Winchester Mystery House 30

The Ghost of Anne Boleyn 36

Haunting Facts....................42

Quiz 44

Activity....................45

Glossary 46

Read More 47

Internet Sites....................47

Index 48

HAUNTS AND HORRORS

Screams in the night. Strange whispers from empty rooms. Chains rattling in the dark.

Many believe that ghosts exist among us. Sometimes these spirits are angry with those left behind. They may have unfinished business. Others simply can't move on, and walk the places they knew best in life.

A beheaded queen, stately White House spirits, a demon pig with red eyes, a witch with a **vendetta** . . . These are just a few of the ghostly **apparitions** that have mysteriously appeared to frighten people over the years. Do these ghosts and haunted places truly exist? Or are they just **figments** of people's imaginations? The legends of these tales aren't always clear. Read on and find out . . . if you dare.

vendetta: a grudge or fight between two people or groups that has lasted a very long time

apparition: the mysterious figure of a person, often a spirit or dead person

figment: something that only exists in a person's mind

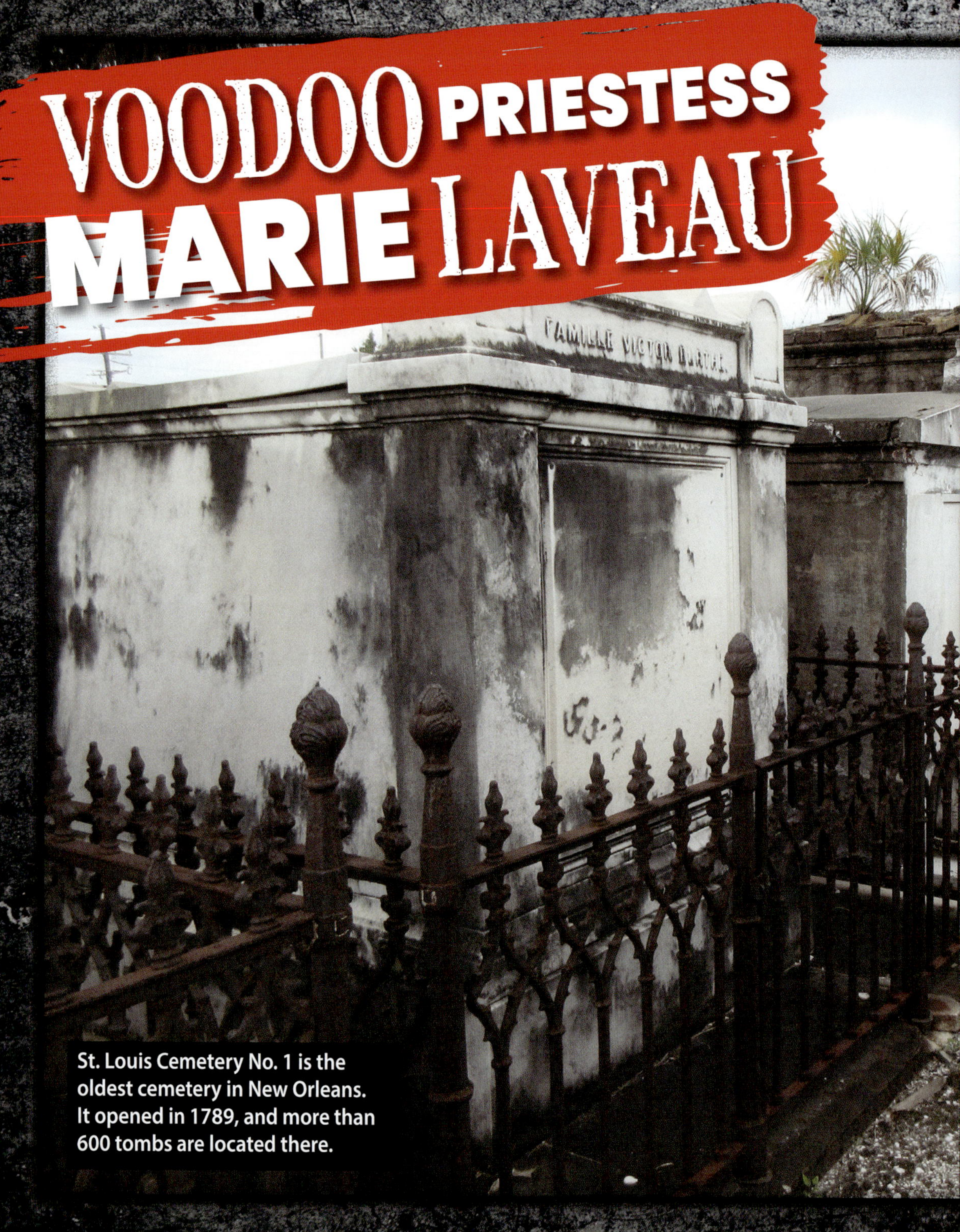

VOODOO PRIESTESS MARIE LAVEAU

St. Louis Cemetery No. 1 is the oldest cemetery in New Orleans. It opened in 1789, and more than 600 tombs are located there.

A man stumbled into the cemetery. He had no home, and he needed a place to sleep. The **tombs**, set aboveground, gleamed a ghostly white. The man curled up on top of one and fell asleep. Then in the dead of night, he woke with a start. Drumbeats filled the air. He had been alone in the cemetery. But suddenly, figures swarmed around him. They parted, and he saw that they were dancing around a tall woman. She had a large snake draped around her neck. The woman was Marie Laveau, Voodoo queen of New Orleans. The man had fallen asleep on her tomb, and she was not pleased.

tomb: a building or chamber built to house a dead body

VOODOO QUEEN

Marie Laveau was a mysterious but well-known figure in New Orleans during the 1800s. Her first husband disappeared after only a year of marriage. Marie was a Voodoo **priestess** and healer. People from all walks of life would go to her for help and advice. She helped those who were sick or in need, but many said that she could also put curses on people. Marie had a big snake. It represented a serpent spirit worshiped in the Voodoo tradition. Legend says she would wear him draped around her neck during Voodoo rituals.

Marie was born in 1801, and was 79 years old when she died.

Snakes are sacred animals to the followers of Voodoo.

priestess: a female religious leader or person of power

After Marie died, many claimed to have seen her still walking the streets of New Orleans, just as she had in life. Even today, some say that she appears as a black cat with glowing eyes. Others say that she appears once a year on St. John's Eve, June 23, an important date in the Voodoo tradition.

In the Voodoo tradition, black cats are thought to be very powerful.

MEETING MARIE

One night about 40 years after her death, Marie appeared in a shop. The shopkeeper was frightened and quickly ran to the back of the store. "Don't you know me?" she asked a customer. He didn't. Marie slapped him and then **levitated** in the air. The customer saw her float out the door and over the walls of a cemetery. He was so scared that he passed out! The shopkeeper revived the customer and told him, "That was Marie Laveau." The customer would not forget her name after that.

Louisiana Voodoo

Voodoo is a set of religious beliefs and practices. It came to the United States when African people were brought there as slaves. Voodoo was also influenced by Catholicism. Voodoo uses charms and herbs called *gris-gris* that can hurt or heal people. Voodoo **practitioners** who are considered powerful are called "queens" and "kings." Sometimes they try to reach otherworldly spirits. These spirits could be gods or demons. Sometimes they are people's long-dead ancestors. Marie Laveau was the most famous Voodoo queen of New Orleans.

Today many people visit Marie's tomb in St. Louis Cemetery No. 1. Visitors continue to ask Marie for her help even after her death. They mark her crypt with three Xs and knock three times. They also leave food, flowers, and other offerings on her tomb. Is Marie a kindly ghost, or a more **malevolent** spirit? Just like when she was alive, there are many rumors, and no one can be sure.

levitate: to rise into the air as if by magic

practitioner: a person who performs an activity or participates in certain religious practices regularly

malevolent: having a desire to hurt someone

WHITE HOUSE GHOSTS

John Adams, the second US president, and his wife Abigail moved into the White House when it was built in 1800. Today people still see Abigail's ghost hanging laundry in the East Room.

It was 1946, and the President of the United States, Harry Truman, had gone to bed early. But a few hours after he had fallen asleep, loud knocks on his bedroom door awakened him. He opened the door and peered into the darkness. No one was there. He walked down the hall to investigate. He looked into the other bedrooms, but saw no one. He turned to go back to his room. Suddenly he heard footsteps in one of the empty rooms he had passed. He looked inside. Nothing.

President Truman returned to his room. In the morning, he talked with the **Secret Service**. They told him no guard would have been in that wing of the White House at that hour. He had been alone . . . Or had he?

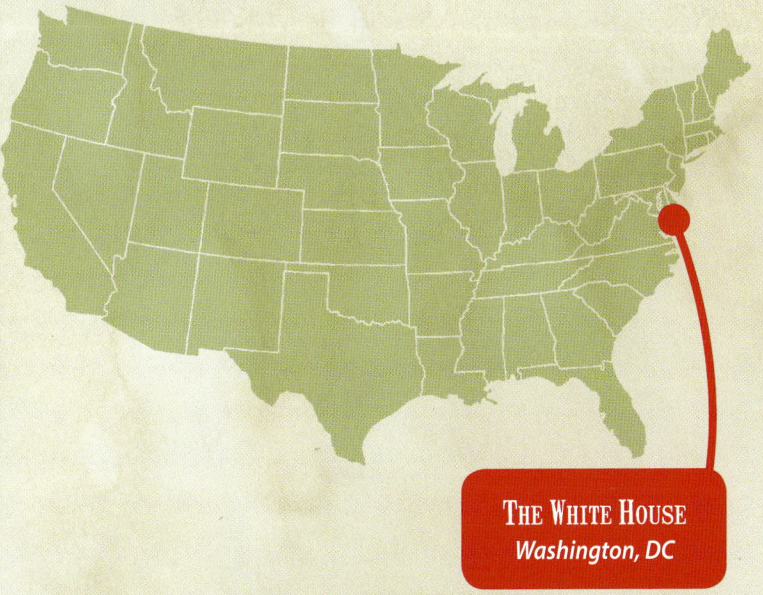

Secret Service: a department of the US government in charge of protecting US leaders, such as the president

A MIDNIGHT VISITOR

Queen Wilhelmina of the Netherlands was staying at the White House for a state visit. She slept in a bedroom that used to be President Abraham Lincoln's office. It was 1942, four years before eerie knocks awakened President Truman in the same room. Around midnight, Queen Wilhelmina heard a knock at her door. She went to open it. This time, someone was there. The queen saw a tall bearded gentleman wearing a top hat. At the sight of the ghost of Abraham Lincoln, the queen fainted. By the time she was revived, the ghostly figure had disappeared.

Queen Wilhelmina of the Netherlands had a strong interest in trying to contact ghosts.

The White House is home to many ghosts, but President Lincoln is seen the most often. He wanders the hallways and knocks on doors. He looks out of windows at what were once Civil War battlefields, across the Potomac River. It is said that Lincoln is more likely to appear during times of trouble—times when the country needs a strong leader the most.

President Lincoln met often with his generals during the Civil War. About 620,000 Americans died during the war, which lasted from 1861 to 1865.

YOUNG GHOSTS

When President Lincoln was alive, he also saw ghosts. His wife, Mary Todd Lincoln, often held **séances** in the White House. They started as a way to contact her young son Willie after his death. "Willie lives," she told her husband and friends. She claimed Willie would come to the foot of her bed almost every night. He appeared to President Lincoln too. The ghost of the young boy was sighted for more than 100 years. Mary also saw the ghost of President Andrew Jackson stomping up and down the corridors and swearing.

séance: a meeting or gathering where people try to make contact with spirits of the dead

Séances

In modern séances, mediums might use Tarot cards or a Ouija board. An object belonging to the dead person may also help them make contact with the dead.

In the mid-1800s, séances were very popular. Many people believed that ghosts could be contacted. During the Civil War, their popularity grew. Many people wanted to speak with their loved ones who had died. People hired **mediums** to communicate with these spirits. Some mediums claimed to speak directly to ghosts. Others interpreted mysterious knocks or noises. Some mediums tricked people—they couldn't really communicate with the dead. But others were more convincing. They knew details that only a ghost could know.

Not all of the White House's unearthly inhabitants are well-known. The ghost of an unknown boy appeared during President William Taft's presidency (1909–1913). They called it "the Thing." The boy would appear behind them and place a hand on their shoulders. President Taft didn't want the story to be revealed to the public. He threatened to fire any staff member who talked about the ghost.

medium: a person who says they can communicate with spirits of the dead

THE AMITYVILLE HAUNTING

Today the Amityville house on Ocean Avenue has a new address to keep tourists away . . . Or is it to protect them from what lies within?

It was 1975. The Lutz family raced down the steps of their house in Amityville, New York, to the waiting car. They had each grabbed only a few changes of clothes to bring with them. They had to get out of there, fast! George Lutz hit the gas, and they sped off into the night. Not even a month earlier, they had been so happy to move in. But the house came with a horrible past. It had been the scene of a brutal **mass murder** just the year before. The family moved in anyway—the house had been very cheap. But only 28 days after moving in, they fled for their lives.

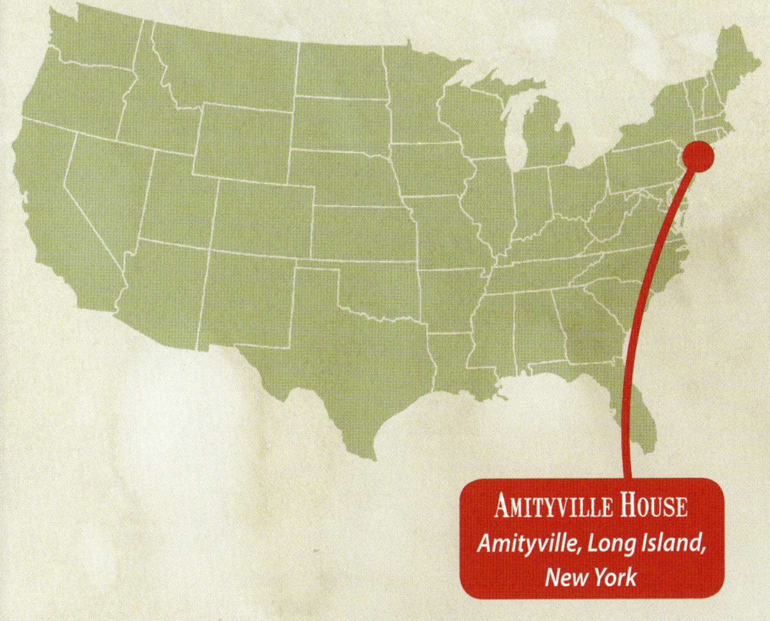

mass murder: the murder of a large number of people

A NEW FRIEND

Missy Lutz was five years old. Missy told her mom and stepdad that her new friend "Jodie" visited her room at night. They thought Jodie was an imaginary friend. They didn't pay much attention at first. One night, George went upstairs to check on Missy. She pointed out the window where Jodie had just left. George turned out the light, but something caught his eye out the window. It was Jodie! She was an enormous pig with glowing red eyes. As George cried out, Jodie disappeared.

Sometimes Jodie appeared to the family as two glowing red eyes.

Green slime oozed out of the walls in the Amityville house. At first, the family thought the kids were making a mess, until it kept happening.

Other strange things happened in the house. One room was full of flies, even in the middle of winter. Strange smells drifted through the hallways. One night, George woke and saw his wife floating over the bed. Green slime oozed out of the walls and through an attic door. George woke up at 3:15 every morning—the same time the murders had taken place.

During an exorcism, a Catholic priest tries to rid a person or place of demons. They use holy water and a crucifix or cross, and say prayers.

TIME TO LEAVE

Father Ray knocked on the door of the Amityville house. Because of the house's past, friends had suggested the family have it **blessed**. The priest was sprinkling holy water in one of the rooms when he felt a chill. Something was wrong with that room. Then he heard a low voice saying "Get out!" An invisible force slapped Father Ray.

bless: to say a prayer to make something holy or to protect it

After the Lutz family fled Amityville, **paranormal** investigators arrived to examine the house. Professional ghost hunters use many different tools in their search for paranormal activity. They take sound and video recordings. Cameras are equipped with night vision and are also able to reveal different areas of hot and cold air. Electromagnetic frequency meters show any irregular **electromagnetic waves**. Even a compass and a thermometer can help them look for ghosts!

paranormal: strange events or phenomenon that cannot be explained by science

electromagnetic wave: a ripple of energy created by electricity and magnetism

Startled Father Ray returned downstairs to the family. "You must never sleep in that room," he told them. And then he left. Later he realized he needed to warn the family more. He tried to call them. But the call was full of static and other strange noises. He was never able to reach them.

But the Lutz family couldn't handle the creepy noises and weird smells. They sold the house and never returned. The new owners are often awakened in the middle of the night—but by tourists and ghost hunters, not spirits. Whatever haunts the Amityville house seems to be quiet . . . for now.

THE BELL WITCH

There are many stories of witches in the United States. During the Salem witch trials (1692–1693), around 200 people were accused of witchcraft.

John Bell looked out over his fields. He had almost forgotten the failed harvests that had brought his family to Tennessee years earlier. Their farmland had grown, as had their family. Now John's daughter Betsy was engaged to be married! The Bell family had truly prospered. There was no reason why that summer in 1817 should be any different.

Strange movements caught John's eye. Striding over to investigate, he hefted his rifle up to his shoulder. A sudden shiver snaked its way down his spine. He couldn't believe what he was seeing. There in the shadows appeared an animal with the body of a dog and the head of a rabbit. John lifted his gun and fired. The animal disappeared.

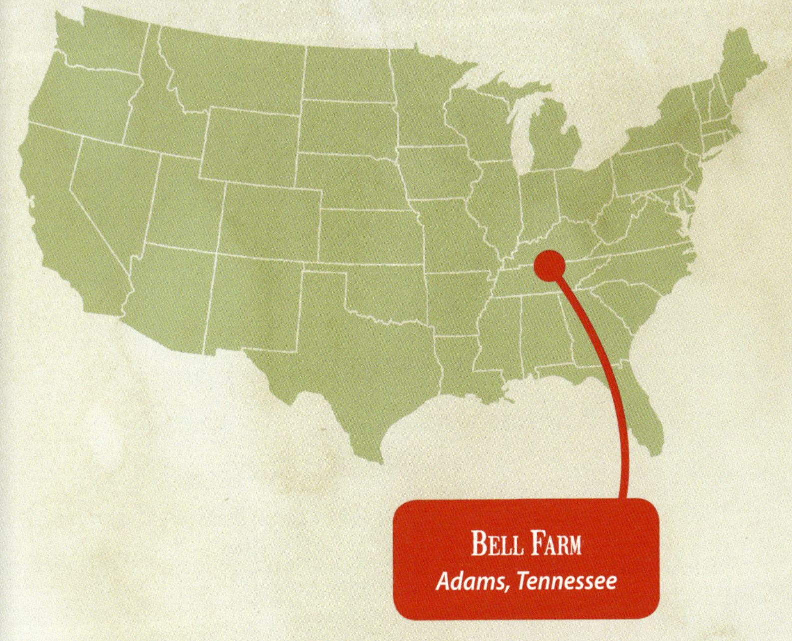

THE GHOST AWAKENS

John's family didn't believe him. But soon they started to see strange things around the property too. Late one night, the family was awakened by unearthly noises—chains dragging across the floor, unexplained knocks from behind the walls. Unseen rats gnawed on the bedposts and kept them awake.

Night after night, the noises continued. They were getting louder. The Bells started to hear choking sounds. Scratchy whispers drifted from every corner of the cabin. An invisible force shook beds and rattled furniture. The malevolent presence seemed to be getting stronger. One night, a woman's voice woke the family. The ghost could talk.

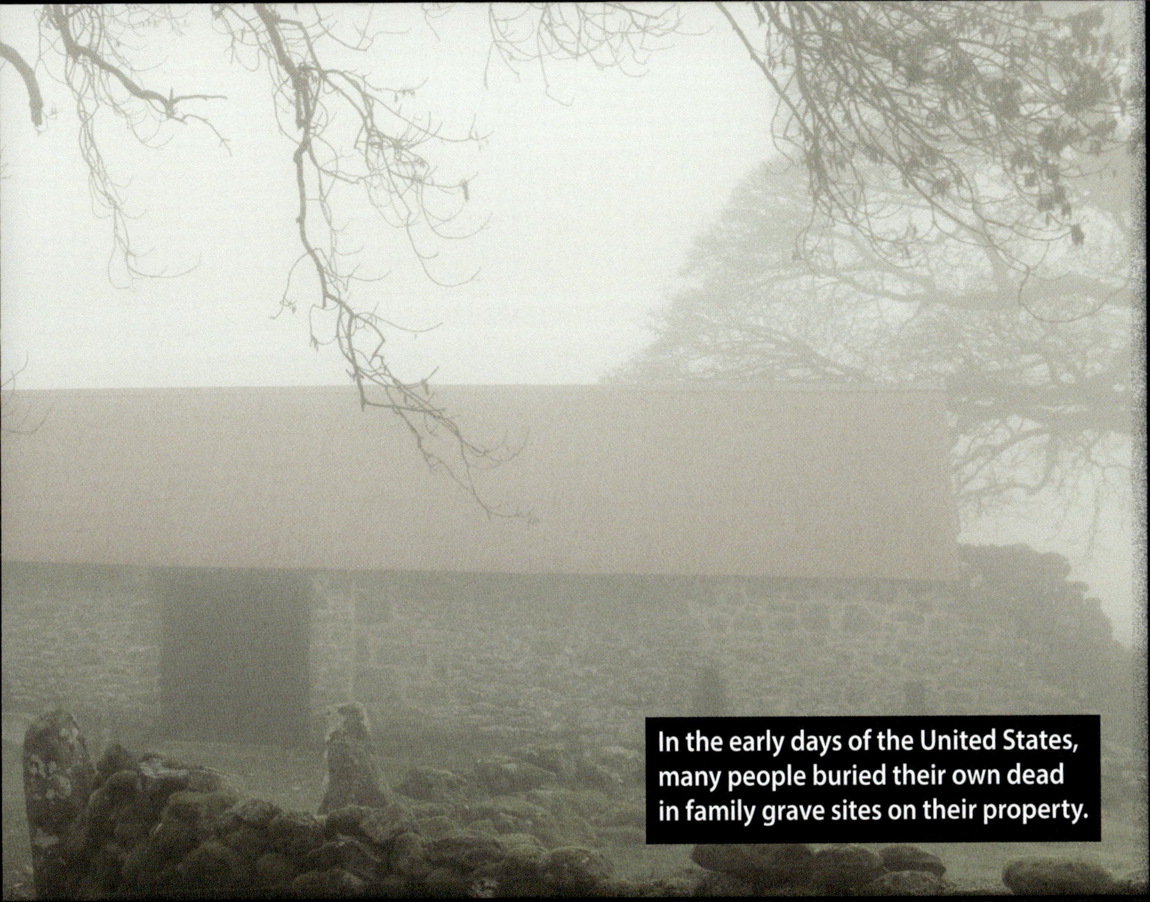

In the early days of the United States, many people buried their own dead in family grave sites on their property.

The Bell Witch, as she came to be known, threatened to kill John many times. He thought the ghost might be his **eccentric** old neighbor, Kate Batts. She had been furious with him when she died. On her deathbed, she threatened to haunt him and his family. Kate's ghost may have returned to drive him to his grave.

eccentric: behaving in strange or unusual ways

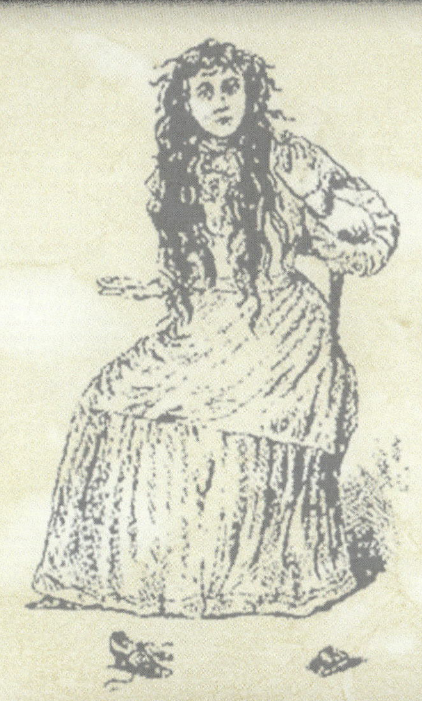

REVENGE

The haunting went on for years. John's health got worse and worse. One night, he reached for his medicine, but the normal bottle had been replaced with a strange **vial**. John was so ill that he didn't notice. He swallowed the liquid anyway. John died just a few hours later. It seemed he had been poisoned. No one in the family knew where the mysterious vial had come from.

After John's death, the witch continued to haunt the family. She didn't want Betsy to get married for some reason. Betsy finally called off her engagement. It seemed like the witch had finally won.

After that, the Bell Witch disappeared . . . for seven years. In 1828, she returned for a few weeks. She told John's son of many things that would happen in the future. She correctly predicted several events of the Civil War. The witch warned the family that she would return in 107 years. But no one knows if she did, or when she will return next . . .

The Bell Witch Cave

At the edge of John Bell's property, there is a cave. Many believe the Bell Witch hid there after tormenting the family. Some believe the witch still appears and disappears from the cave. Visitors have reported feeling heavy weights pushing down on them. They've felt as if they were being squeezed so tightly they couldn't breathe. Mysterious noises and lights continue to come from the cave to this day.

vial: a small container that usually holds liquid medicine

Almost 20 percent of people in the United States report that they have seen a ghost.

WINCHESTER MYSTERY HOUSE

Holding a person's hand is one way that mediums claim to receive information from ghosts or spirits.

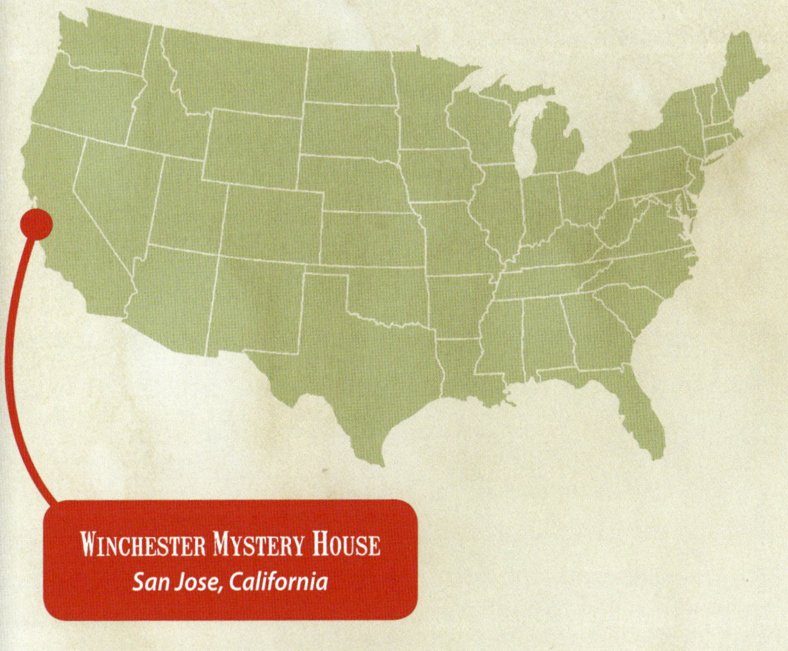

Candles flickered in the darkened room. The medium reached out for the hand of the woman across from her. Sarah Winchester paused for a moment, taking a shuddery breath before placing her hand in the medium's.

Sarah's life had been marked by tragedy. Her infant daughter had died in 1866, and her husband passed on 15 years later. Alone and grieving, Sarah had hoped the medium would be able to contact her child and husband from beyond the grave. "He's here!" the medium cried out. She described the man that Sarah had hoped to see, but the message wasn't one she wanted to hear.

A GRAVE WARNING

Sarah's husband was William Wirt Winchester, heir to a fortune made by selling rifles. His ghost told the medium that there was a curse on the family. He spoke of the angry ghosts of people who had died after being shot by the guns he sold. The medium told Sarah there was only one way to protect herself. She had to build a house to confuse the angry spirits. If Sarah ever stopped building, she would die.

Sarah Winchester

Parts of the Winchester Mystery House can be toured today. In 2017, 40 additional rooms were opened to the public.

Sarah fled the séance and began to do what the medium had instructed. She sold her family home in Connecticut and headed west. When she arrived in California, Sarah purchased a large farmhouse. She immediately hired construction crews to work all through the day and night.

Construction happened quickly and continuously. There was no time to make blueprints. Sarah designed the house herself—with a little supernatural help. Every evening, she would go into her private séance room and ask spirits about the next day's construction.

The Winchester house was seven stories tall before the top three levels collapsed in an earthquake in 1906.

UNEXPLAINED ADDITIONS

Soon the house sprawled out like a maze. Stairways spiraled up and led to nothing. Doors opened onto brick walls. Hallways zigged and zagged. The house reached seven stories tall. Sarah built secret passages and trapdoors. People unfamiliar with the house quickly became lost, but few people other than the construction crew or the servants ever entered it.

No one knows why, but Sarah was fascinated by the number 13. She designed rooms with 13 windows. Stairways had 13 steps. Maybe she hoped it was a lucky number that would help protect her. Construction continued at a feverish pace. It seemed that Sarah had managed to escape the vengeful spirits who would do her harm. Or maybe the curse had worked, and she had already lost everything important to her.

Sarah died peacefully in her bed at the age of 83. Construction finally stopped—38 years after it had begun.

The Winchester House Today

It seems that Sarah Winchester successfully warded off the evil spirits who were haunting her. One of the ghosts who has been sighted the most often in the house appears to be friendly. The ghost appears in white overalls, pushing a wheelbarrow. He is said to haunt the basement of the home. Many believe that he was a former worker on the property, still at work on a project that ended long ago.

The Winchester Mystery House has 950 doors and more than 10,000 windows.

THE GHOST OF ANNE BOLEYN

Construction on parts of the Tower of London started more than 900 years ago. It was used as a military fort before becoming a prison.

One night in 1864, a guard made his nightly patrol in the **Tower of London**. The air was so cold, he could see his breath as he made his rounds. Suddenly, across the courtyard, he saw a tall figure. It looked like a woman in white. The guard approached. How had she gotten into the locked grounds in the middle of the night? The woman turned and charged toward him. The guard lifted his **bayonet** to protect himself. Suddenly he realized the woman was floating. Her feet weren't touching the ground! He thrust the bayonet and it went straight through the woman. She vanished into thin air.

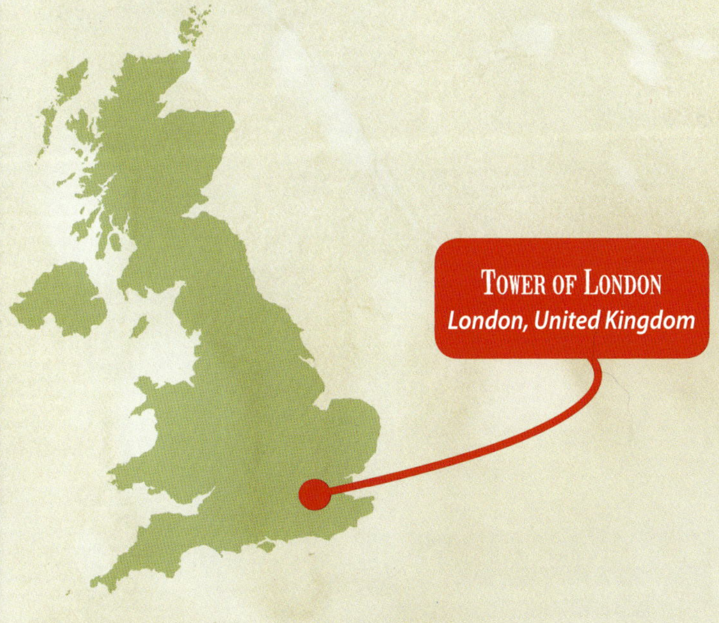

Tower of London: a historic castle in London that was also used as a prison for hundreds of years

bayonet: a long knife attached to the end of a rifle

Members of the Queen's Guard, called Beefeaters, keep watch over the Tower of London. Although it is no longer a prison, the Tower still houses the crown jewels.

A ROYAL GHOST

When the ghostly woman disappeared, the guard fainted in the middle of the courtyard. The other guards found him there. He was brought before the captain and accused of sleeping on duty. He would have been in a lot of trouble if it hadn't been for Major General J.D. Dundas. Dundas had witnessed the whole unearthly scene from one of the towers. He told the men what he had seen. The guard's job was saved. But it took him a while to recover from his fright.

Years later, the captain of the guard saw a strange light flickering in the Chapel Royal. He climbed a ladder to investigate. As he climbed into the tower, he saw a long procession of knights and ladies wearing **Renaissance** clothing. A beautiful young woman was leading the procession. Though he couldn't clearly see her face, the captain recognized her from portraits he had seen of Anne Boleyn. He believed this was the ghost of the second wife of Henry VIII.

Anne Boleyn was **executed** in 1536. Many believe she was falsely accused of crimes because she gave birth to a female heir and not a male one, as Henry VIII had wanted.

execute: to put a condemned criminal to death

Renaissance: a period of time in Europe between the 14th and 17th centuries

In 1674, bones were discovered in the Chapel of St. John in the Tower of London. Experts believe they are the bones of two young princes who were murdered.

A WANDERING SPIRIT

The Tower of London has been home to **treasonous** acts, murders, and executions during its 900-year history. It is no surprise that it is one of the most haunted places in the United Kingdom. The ghost of Anne Boleyn is a frequent visitor. It was there that she was held before her execution by beheading. The guards on duty who came across her ghostly apparition could be considered lucky. They saw Anne appear as a young woman. Others have not been so lucky. Some have seen a headless Anne as she wanders the corridors, carrying her own head in her arms.

treasonous: involving the betrayal of one's own country or government

In 2015, a visitor on a tour to Hever Castle was taking photographs. A few months later, when he looked through the photos, he noticed something weird . . . There was a ghostly hand in one corner of a picture. The hand points toward the chimney in Anne Boleyn's former prayer room. The tourist said he believes Anne Boleyn's ghost was trying to show him that there is something important hidden there.

But Anne Boleyn does not limit her ghostly appearances to the Tower of London. She has been seen all over the UK in various locations that were important to her. Around Christmas every year, it is said that she returns to her family home in Hever Castle.

Sightings of Anne Boleyn's ghost at Hever Castle have been more peaceful than sightings in other locations.

HAUNTING FACTS

MARY LINCOLN also tried to contact the GHOSTS of deceased war generals during her séances. She would ask them for ADVICE about the ongoing Civil War so that she could pass on ideas to her husband.

CLINTON ROAD in New Jersey is said to be a haunted highway. Drivers are warned to be on the lookout for GHOST TRUCKS, CANNIBALS in the woods, and the GHOST OF A BOY that guards a bridge.

The Eastern State Penitentiary in Philadelphia is one of the MOST HAUNTED places in the United States. It closed down as a prison years ago, but visitors still hear unearthly moans, disembodied laughter, and unexplained footsteps.

The LINCOLN PARK ZOO in Chicago isn't just home to animals, but also to GHOSTS, according to paranormal researchers. Lincoln Park used to be the city's LARGEST cemetery, but many of the bodies were moved elsewhere. The zoo was built on top of the old cemetery.

A recent survey found that around 52 PERCENT of Americans believe in GHOSTS.

In ancient times, Romans had a holiday in May called LEMURALIA. During that time, they performed rituals to rid their houses of EVIL GHOSTS.

In 2003, a security camera at one of Henry VIII's homes captured a GHOSTLY HOODED FIGURE in period clothes. It was seen closing fire-escape doors that had swung open mysteriously. The spectral apparition has been dubbed "SKELETOR."

QUIZ

1. Where is Marie Laveau's tomb?

2. Which US president heard a ghost in 1946?

3. Who did people used to hire to communicate with spirits?

4. What are some of the tools that ghost hunters use?

5. What percent of people in the United States report they have seen a ghost?

6. Which number fascinated Sarah Winchester?

7. Where was Anne Boleyn's ghost seen?

8. What happened to Anne Boleyn in 1536?

9. What percent of Americans believe in ghosts?

10. During which ancient Roman holiday did people rid their houses of ghosts?

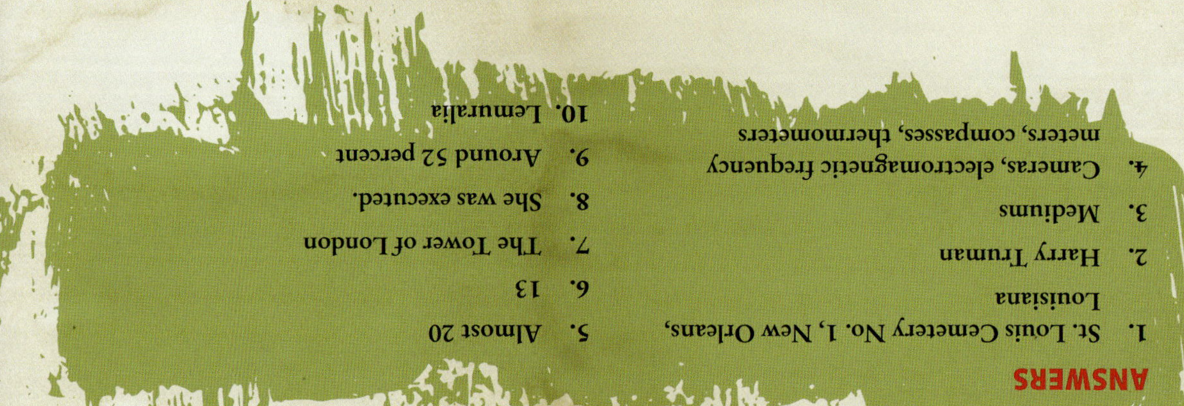

ANSWERS

1. St. Louis Cemetery No. 1, New Orleans, Louisiana
2. Harry Truman
3. Mediums
4. Cameras, electromagnetic frequency meters, compasses, thermometers
5. Almost 20
6. 13
7. The Tower of London
8. She was executed.
9. Around 52 percent
10. Lemuralia

ACTIVITY

Research and write a short story about a haunting near you!

Haunted houses, creepy cemeteries, paranormal prisons . . . What haunted places are located near you? In this activity, you will research a local haunting and write your own ghost story.

MATERIALS NEEDED

- Group of three to four friends or classmates
- Library or internet access
- Pencils and paper

STEPS

1 With your group, research local stories about hauntings in your town or state. Use the internet or library to help you.

2 Pick one story to write about. You can focus on one particular ghost or haunted place.

3 Make a list of the details you found in your research. What do you want to include in your story?

4 Use your imagination to make your story spooky! But back it up with the research you did to keep it accurate.

5 Share the story with your family, other friends, or classmates!

GLOSSARY

apparition: the mysterious figure of a person, often a spirit or dead person

bayonet: a long knife attached to the end of a rifle

bless: to say a prayer to make something holy or to protect it

eccentric: behaving in strange or unusual ways

electromagnetic wave: a ripple of energy created by electricity and magnetism

execute: to put a condemned criminal to death

figment: something that only exists in a person's mind

levitate: to rise into the air as if by magic

malevolent: having a desire to hurt someone

mass murder: the murder of a large number of people

medium: a person who says they can communicate with spirits of the dead

paranormal: strange events or phenomenon that cannot be explained by science

practitioner: a person who performs an activity or participates in certain religious practices regularly

priestess: a female religious leader or person of power

Renaissance: a period of time in Europe between the 14th and 17th centuries

Secret Service: a department of the US government in charge of protecting US leaders, such as the president

séance: a meeting or gathering where people try to make contact with spirits of the dead

tomb: a building or chamber built to house a dead body

Tower of London: a historic castle in London that was also used as a prison for hundreds of years

treasonous: involving the betrayal of one's own country or government

vendetta: a grudge or fight between two people or groups that has lasted a very long time

vial: a small container that usually holds liquid medicine

READ MORE

Johnson, Cheri. *Hauntings.* Origins: Urban Legends. Fremont, Calif.: Full Tilt Press, 2018.

Roza, Greg. *Ossuaries and Charnel Houses.* Digging Up the Dead. New York: Gareth Stevens Publishing, 2015.

Walsh, Liza Gardner. *Ghost Hunter's Handbook: Supernatural Explorations for Kids.* Real-Life Ghost Stories. Lanham, Md: Down East Books, 2016.

Wilkins, Ebony. *Perron Family Haunting: The Ghost Story That Inspired Horror Movies.* North Mankato, Minn.: Snap Books, 2020.

INTERNET SITES

https://academickids.com/encyclopedia/index.php/Voodoo
Explore the history and traditions of the Voodoo religion.

https://kids.kiddle.co/Anne_Boleyn
Read about the life—and death—of Anne Boleyn.

https://kids.nationalgeographic.com/explore/history/salem-witch-trials/
National Geographic explains the events of the Salem Witch Trials.

INDEX

cemeteries 6, 7, 10, 11, 43, 44
Civil War 14, 15, 17, 28, 42

electromagnetic waves 23

Lincoln, Abraham 14, 15, 16, 42
Lutz family 19, 20, 23

mediums 17, 30, 31, 32, 33

New Orleans 6, 7, 8, 9, 10, 11, 44

paranormal investigators 23

Queen Wilhelmina of the Netherlands 14

séances 16, 17, 33, 42

Tower of London 36, 37, 38, 40, 41, 44
Truman, Harry 13, 14, 44

Voodoo 6, 7, 8, 9, 11

White House 5, 12, 13, 14, 16, 17
Winchester, Sarah 30, 31, 32, 33, 34, 35, 44